PICKLING

FOR THE

ABSOLUTE

BEGINNER

The perfect starter book to get you pickling as soon as possible. This is a simple, non-complicated book designed and structured to help the complete beginner with a desire to start pickling, to understand quickly the simple processes.

CARL WILLIAMS

Disclaimer Notice

Please note the information contained within this document is for educational and entertainment purposes only. All effort has been executed to present accurate, up to date, and reliable, complete information. No warranties of any kind are declared or implied. Readers acknowledge that the author is not engaging in the rendering of legal, financial, medical or professional advice. The content within this book has been derived from various sources. Please consult a licensed professional before attempting any techniques outlined in this book.

By reading this document, the reader agrees that under no circumstances is the author responsible for any losses, direct or indirect, which are incurred as a result of the use of the information contained within this document, including, but not limited to, — errors, missions, or inaccuracies.

CONTENTS

INTRODUCTION

Hi Readers. First of all, thank you for buying my book. I have tried to structure this book, and the flow of the words in a way that makes it easy reading; in a way that makes it easy to understand, so that you can very quickly start on your pickling journey.

I have two main passions in life. One is gardening and the other is cooking. I love both.

I love growing food in the garden. Growing herbs, garlic, chillies and many more. Also growing the many fantastic flowers from seed is very rewarding.

I love cooking. Creating a great meal from basic ingredients. There are parallels with both of these passions. Creation. Creating things makes us feel good. Starting with a blank canvas like a plot of land and turning it into a lush garden is similar to starting with basic ingredients and developing a nice meal.

Pickling is a sort of link between the two passions. I can grow vegetables, herbs and chillies in the garden and then I can pickle them in the kitchen to use to compliment any meal.

This book will not cover fermentation – which is another method of preserving food which is similar to pickling however fermentation includes a step where food is soaked in salt water to encourage fermentation where a chemical reaction happens between sugars in the food and naturally present bacteria. Fermentation helps pro-biotics to thrive which is good for digestion.

This book will look at the pickling process, quick pickling, canning, and all the equipment and ingredients that you will need.

Use this book as a starting point for your journey. This book will give you a good understanding of how the pickling method is preserving your food as well as guiding you through the process to make your own pickles. I didn't want to just give you the process and recipes without you understanding how it works.

So.... Use this book as a starting point, but also continue your learning by reading as many books as you can on pickling and also make good use of the many videos available on YouTube. However, when watching YouTube videos you can use your understanding of pickling that you will get from this book to filter the good and bad information in the online world.

CHAPTER ONE – EQUIPMENT

Let's begin. What do you need to get started? You can buy a limited amount of equipment to do basic pickling or quick pickling. However you will need some more equipment if you decide to do canning (a specific method which encourages a longer lasting life for your pickled food)

For basic pickling and quick pickling I advise that you buy and use the following equipment:-

1. **Jars** – You can actually use most types of jars as long as you can get a good seal with the lid. However, I strongly recommend that you buy glass mason Jars. Glass mason jars have three components to them. The Jar, the lid and the band. The advantage of using these types of jars is that you can equally use them for basic pickling/quick pickling and for canning. The lids create a very strong seal with the jar and you can buy additional lids in the future when your current lids get old and show signs of wear and tear.

2. **Saucepan for pickling liquid** – In order to combine and heat your pickling liquid ingredients you will need a non-reactive pan which basically means a stainless steel, glass or enamelled saucepan. This is

because other pans can react with the acids or salts in the liquid.

3. **Saucepan to sterilise your jars** – This could be the same type of saucepan that you use for the pickling liquid however this saucepan usually needs to be quite large to completely submerge your jars, lids, bands and any other utensils that need to be sterilised. Remember the importance of everything being sterile to prevent any bacteria from forming.

4. **Jar lifting tongues** – These can be very useful for lifting your jars in and out of the boiling water during the sterilisation process. Without the tongues this can be very tricky and also potentially dangerous due to the boiling water. Therefore I strongly advise that you invest in some good quality lifting tongues.

5. **Funnel** – A stainless steel funnel (also sterilised) is a very handy tool for pickling. You can use it to add the pickling liquid to the jars without spillage and keeping the outside of the jars clean.

The sterilisation process

It's important to point out the sterilisation process.

- Bring a large saucepan filled with water to the boil.
- Add everything that needs to be sterilised. The jars, the lids, the bands, any utensils that may come into contact with the jars.
- Allow the water to simmer for 10 minutes

- Remove the jars, lids etc from the pan using the tongues and ensure they are kept clean before using them. Time it so that you are almost ready to fill the jars with your pickling ingredients soon after sterilisation.

CHAPTER TWO – INGREGIENTS

Great – you now have all the equipment you need. But what ingredients do you need? Well firstly you need the food that you are trying to pickle. For example, onions or cucumber or eggs etc etc. The list goes on.........................

Then, you need the pickling liquid. The pickling liquid is where the magic happens. Not only does it add flavour but more importantly it is the pickling liquid that preserves the food and keeps it safe. I will go into more detail about the pickling liquid later in this book but the basic ingredients for most pickling liquids are:-

1. Vinegar with at least 5% acidity (This is essential.) You can use distilled white vinegar or malt vinegar (usually used for making pickled onions.) However the important point is to ensure that your vinegar is at least 5% acidic.
2. Salt. Use sea salt of Kosher salt. Try to avoid table salt as they can contain iodine or anti caking agents.
3. Sugar. Many pickling liquids contain sugar which are mainly added for flavour.
4. Water. Simple tab water forms part of the pickling liquid with the ratio to vinegar changing for different recipes. I will cover this later in the book.
5. Whole spices. These are not essential for preserving the food however they can be added for flavour.

Whole spices like peppercorns, mustard seeds and coriander seeds make a great addition to your pickling jar. Avoid powdered spices as they will cloud your pickling liquid

6. Fresh herbs and garlic/chillies. Fresh herbs like dill are also a great addition to your pickles and also adding a clove of garlic or even some fresh chillies will add incredible flavour and heat if you like it spicy.

CHAPTER THREE – THE LIQUID

Right, we have reached the exciting part where the magic happens. The liquid, or the brine is the most important part of pickling. This liquid is not only about flavour. This liquid, using the correct ratio of vinegar to water is what actually preserves the food and makes it safe.

You can read lots of books and watch many videos on this and you can feel like you understand it. Then you may see a recipe in a book or online and immediately feel like you don't understand it at all as the recipe you are looking at contradicts what you have previously learnt.

Actually it is quite simple. The vinegar does all the work. Most recipes use a 50% to 50% ratio of water to vinegar. Meaning that vinegar and water will be equal. For example 250ml of Vinegar and 250ml of water. Salt is important and is added and help to make the liquid better for preservation however it is the vinegar that does all the work.

To put it simply. You can entirely use vinegar and omit the water. Water is added to help with taste by diluting the vinegar down which people can find quite harsh. Pickled onions are one example that often uses 100% vinegar with no water. However many recipes that you will see in books and online will use 50% water and 50% vinegar to help with flavour by reducing the harsh taste of vinegar.

So if you are seeing many different recipes in books or online that use different ratios of water to vinegar it is because they are considering taste and flavour whilst also considering the most import part which is ensuring the liquid has enough vinegar to preserve the food.

You can always increase the vinegar to water ratio and it will keep the food safe, but you must not reduce the ratio of vinegar to water as this can be dangerous.

Vinegar should be at least 50% for the liquid. It can be higher than 50%. It can be 100%, but don't let it fall below 50%.

A word about PH. Your liquid should be highly acidic. If you use the ratios correctly, as described in this book, using at least 50% vinegar to water then your liquid will be highly acidic.

However, you can test this. A highly acidic liquid will have a PH value of 4.6 or lower. You can purchase a PH meter or PH strips to test the acidity of your liquid.

DO NOT BE SCARED – follow the recipes and you will be fine. Pickling is fun and people have been doing it for many many years. However being aware of the important ratios mentioned in this book will give you a better understanding of the process.

CHAPTER FOUR – THE PICKLING PROCESS

The basic pickling process is actually quite simple. Just remember the points I have made in this book about sterilising all equipment.

Remember the rules about the liquid ratios (vinegar is king,) and remember the importance of a strong seal between the jar and the lid.

There is a chapter in this book talking about the process of canning which is a method that encourages a longer life for your pickled jars but first we will talk about the basic pickling process.

1. Choose what you want to pickle. I advise you to pickle foods that you already see pickled in supermarkets etc. For example, onions, eggs, cucumber, gherkin.
2. Sterilise your equipment, utensils etc. etc. as describes previously.
3. Make the liquid.
   a. Get a no-reactive saucepan and add vinegar, water, salt and sugar to the pan (use the ratios given to you in a recipe, but if you are making a 500ml liquid you can use 250ml vinegar to 250ml water with 50g of kosher salt and 200g of sugar. Remember you can increase the percentage of vinegar but don't reduce it. If you are pickling onions it is normal to use 100% malt vinegar. Therefore, using this example

you would add 500ml of vinegar with 50g of kosher salt and 200g of sugar.

    b. Bring the liquid to a boil

4. Prepare your jars.

    a. Place the food of your choice (for example onions) into the jars to fill the jars leaving a gap at the top.

    b. Add anything extra that you want to add flavour. For example, a garlic clove, a fresh chilli, some whole spices like peppercorns, coriander seeds or mustard seeds.

    c. Pour the hot liquid, using a funnel, into the jars making sure that you don't have any air pockets. Fill the jar with the liquid leaving approximately a one centimetre gap between the liquid and the top of the jar.

Make sure that the liquid covers all of the food.

d. Add the lid to the jar and then put the band on and tighten the band. Do not over tighten the band.

You are done. You now have a jar of food contained in an air tight sterilised jar which is covered by a liquid containing enough vinegar to preserve the food. This jar could last a long time if you don't open it. Once you open it you must refrigerate the jar and eat within a few weeks.

Quick Pickling

I just want to briefly talk about quick pickling. You will read and see videos about quick pickling and it can be confusing. Quick pickling is describes as a method for beginners that is easy to make but the jars must be refrigerated and only last a few weeks.

However, you will probably see some quick pickle recipes that look exactly the same in method as I have described in this book. Meaning that the correct ratio of vinegar has been used and the jar is sealed correctly.

Therefore, my opinion is that quick pickling is about making pickles that you intend to eat within a few weeks.

If the jar lid is coming off and on regularly then it is a good idea to store in the fridge and eat within a few weeks. However, some recipes may be in the category of quick pickling but they can also be perfect for long term storage, assuming that the lid is kept on the jar.

Just remember one thing. If your finished jar of pickled food has the right ratio of vinegar; has a lid that has a perfect seal; and the jar is completely sterilised then your food will last a long time on the shelf.

Methods like canning, explained later encourage the above conditions. Boiling the filled jars in water guarantees sterilisation and will kill any bacteria and will help to create a better seal with the lid.

CHAPTER FIVE – CANNING

Canning, or water bath canning is a method used to encourage a longer life for the pickled jars you have created. It is important be know that you must use Mason Jars that I recommended at the beginning of this book for the canning method.

You need a large pan. The hight of the pan needs to be higher than your jars because the jars have to be completely below the water line by at least one inch. Therefore make sure your pan is high enough. Alternatively you can buy specific canning pots that have a rack on the bottom to keep the jars off the bottom of the pan

This process involves bringing water to a boil in the pan and then adding your sealed filled mason jars (containing your food and liquid etc) to the boiling water. The jars normally sit on a rack keeping them off the bottom of the pan. Make sure that the jars are fully submerged in the water (at least one inch below the water level.)

Follow any recipe to see how long you should boil the jars for, however a usual rule of thumb is to boil the water containing the jars for at least 10 minutes.

After the recommended time has elapsed you can remover the jars using your tongues and let them cool on the worktop.

CHAPTER SIX – SAFETY

I mentioned earlier not to be scared about pickling. Pickling has been a method of preserving food for a very long time and you should enjoy pickling.

If you keep to the important rules about sterilisation, and keep to the correct ratios of vinegar to water, and achieve a good seal between the lid and jar then your pickles will be perfectly good to eat. Choosing to use the canning method should guarantee that this is achieved.

However it is good practice to check your jars after you open them for any signs of spoilage. Use your instincts. If the product does not smell right then trust your instincts. Look for any evidence that bacteria has grown. Check your jars. Make sure that no cracks have emerged. Check for swelling, bulging or leaking from the lid.

Due to bacteria causing a build-up of gas, if you notice and liquid squirting out when you open the jar then discard the product and do not eat it.

If the food is mouldy, discoloured, does not smell right or the lid is swelling or bulging then do not take any chances. DO NOT EAT IT.

CHAPTER SEVEN – A FEW SIMPLE RECIPES

- **<u>Spicy Pickled Onions</u>**

Ingredients

500g of small shallot

50g salt

500ml malt vinegar (remember vinegar needs to be at least 5% acidic)

200g sugar

Fresh chillies (quantity to own taste)

Garlic clove (pealed)

Peppercorn (small handful)

Mustard Seeds (small handful)

Chilli flakes (to taste)

Method

1. After pealing the onions pour salt all over them in a bowl and leave them overnight to allow the salt to extract moisture from the onions (this will help in the preserving process but also make the onions more crunchy.)
2. The day later rinse all the salt off the onions.
3. Create the liquid. In a pan add the salt, vinegar and sugar and bring to the boil.
4. Fill the jars. After the jars have been sterilised, fill the jars with the onions, fresh dill, a few chillies, a clove of garlic, a few chilli flakes (not powder,) mustard seeds and peppercorns, and pour in the vinegar based liquid.

5. Put the lid on the jar and tighten the band.

- **Pickled Eggs**

Ingredients

  6 – 8 boiled eggs

  50g salt

  500ml white distilled vinegar (remember vinegar needs to be at least 5% acidic)

  200g sugar

Method

  1 Hard boil the eggs in water for 10 minutes. Remove from the pan and allow to cool. Once cooled remove the egg shells.
  2 Create the liquid. In a pan add the salt, vinegar and sugar and bring to the boil.

3 Fill the jars. After the jars have been sterilised, fill the jars with the peeled, cooked eggs then pour in the vinegar based liquid.
4 Put the lid on the jar and tighten the band.

- **<u>Spicy Cucumber</u>**

Ingredients

1 Whole Cucumber

50g salt

500ml distilled white vinegar (remember vinegar needs to be at least 5% acidic)

200g sugar

Fresh chillies (quantity to own taste)

Garlic clove (pealed)

Peppercorn (small handful)

Mustard Seeds (small handful)

Chilli flakes (to taste)

Method

1 Cut the cucumber into thin slices then place in a bowl. Sprinkle the cucumber with salt and leave overnight.

2 The day later rinse all the salt off the cucumber.

3 Create the liquid. In a pan add the salt, vinegar and sugar and bring to the boil.

4 Fill the jars. After the jars have been sterilised, fill the jars with the cucumber, fresh dill, a few chillies, garlic, chilli flakes (not powder), mustard seeds and peppercorns, and pour in the vinegar based liquid.

5 Put the lid on the jar and tighten the band.

CONCLUSION

Thank you for reading this book. I hope you find it useful and I hope it helps you on your way to becoming a pickling expert.

Treat this book as a starting point that will begin your journey, but also do as much research from other sources to grow your knowledge. Also use other books, social media and videos to help you.

I hope pickling gives you as much pleasure and satisfaction as it does for me. Don't be scared. Start today and see the great rewards it can give you.

Made in United States
Troutdale, OR
12/08/2024

26149076R00022